USS Constitution
Old Ironsides

Photography by Steve Dunwell

Introduction by William M. Fowler, Jr.

Preface by Charles Francis Adams

An American eagle carved into the gangway board greets visitors as they step onto the deck of "Old Ironsides."

PREFACE

*This book is intended
to give those who visit Old Ironsides,
and the museum that goes with her,
a highly readable text,
together with a fine array of photographs
to enhance the experience.
For those who may be considering a visit to this
extraordinary old ship, this book should serve to draw interest
and attention to the remarkable experience such a visit affords.
As one stands on the deck of USS Constitution
and views her gun battery and the tall rig
that brought it into action, one is moved to feel a desire
to learn more about the ship, her campaigns,
and the men who served on her.
Steve Dunwell and William M. Fowler, Jr.,
do full justice to the fascinating story of this great ship.
It is a source of great satisfaction to write these lines,
for my family have been interested in USS Constitution
since her launching in 1797 during the
presidency of John Adams.*

Charles Francis Adams
Boston, Massachusetts
January 1991

Overleaf: *Constitution's* lofty masts and miles of rigging are silhouetted against the skyline of Boston.

INTRODUCTION

USS *Constitution* is the oldest commissioned warship afloat in the world. She was commissioned by our first president, George Washington, and launched in the administration of our second president, John Adams.

During the first decade of American independence, the new republic faced serious threats from enemies abroad. In the Mediterranean, for example, our merchant vessels were being seized by the Barbary corsairs. These seagoing extortionists had for generations sortied out of their bases in North Africa to attack any merchantmen daring to venture close to their shores. In the years before our Revolution, vessels from America had sailed under the protection of the Royal Navy. With independence, however, we were on our own. Americans were outraged that their ships were being seized and their crews imprisoned. A rising public chorus demanded that President Washington and the Congress take action to protect American lives and property.

On 27 March, 1794, President Washington signed "an act to provide a naval armament." This legislation authorized the construction of four 44-gun and two 36-gun ships. To appease those in the Congress who were fearful of creating an expensive naval establishment, a proviso was added to the legislation that should a peace be negotiated with the Barbary states, then "no further proceeding be had under this act." Early in 1796 just such a peace was achieved. President Washington, however, convinced that the nation ought not to be defenseless at sea, persuaded Congress to allow the completion of three of the planned six frigates: *Constellation* at Baltimore, *United States* at Philadelphia, and *Constitution* at Boston.

Constitution's keel was laid in the spring of 1795 in the yard of Edmund Hartt. Neither Mr. Hartt nor any other shipbuilder in Boston had ever built a vessel this large. Just gathering sufficient materials for construction proved to be an arduous task. Live oak, carefully chosen for its strength, was brought up from the South for frames and planking. Pine came down from Maine for spars. Dozens of carpenters, caulkers, riggers, and other skilled workmen swarmed around the frigate while Bostonians came to gawk at this wooden giant rising on their waterfront.

On 21 October, 1797, amidst cheering crowds, salutes fired by militiamen, and innumerable toasts, *Constitution* slid into the water. Carefully, her crew brought her to the fitting-out dock. For the next several months workmen labored to step her masts and prepare the frigate for sea. All hands were aboard on 22 July, 1798, when *Constitution,* under the command of Samuel Nicholson, hoisted sail, dropped down the harbor, and after taking the salute from the Castle, laid a course for the open sea and then south toward the West Indies. Her log records the moment:

> Steady Breezes fine and Pleasant Weather. At 8 p.m. Took my departure from Boston Light House bearing W ½ N 3½ Leagues dist.

Constitution made two voyages under Nicholson. On both cruises her mission was to defend American commerce against attacks from French privateers and men-of-war. Although France had been our ally in the struggle for American independence, by 1798 the French had undergone their own revolution and were embroiled in war with Great Britain. The United States remained

neutral in this battle between the two European giants. Unhappy that her former ally refused to help her, the French government authorized attacks on American ships in retaliation. Thus was born the "Quasi War," an undeclared naval war with France.

Captain Nicholson was a disappointment. He was a crusty and irascible sort, and within a few weeks of taking command, the "Commodore" managed to antagonize his officers, his crew, and the secretary of the navy. To no one's dismay or surprise, at the end of his second voyage in May 1799, Nicholson stepped aside to allow a new captain, Silas Talbot, aboard.

Silas Talbot was a hero of the Revolution. Hailing from Rhode Island, he had served in both the Continental army and navy and had been wounded several times. Under his command *Constitution* made its presence felt. Ably assisted by his first lieutenant, Isaac Hull, Talbot soon sent French rascals and others who were preying on American trade scurrying for safety.

While Talbot and his frigate prowled the waters near the islands of Cuba and Hispaniola, American and French diplomats in Paris worked to end the "war." Neither side had a desire to prolong the affair, and after some months of negotiations, the Senate ratified a treaty of peace on 2 March 1801. Two days later Thomas Jefferson was inaugurated president.

The new president was a frugal man, and with peace he saw little need of a navy. Sensing what was to come, Silas Talbot resigned from the navy in September 1801. His frigate was placed in the hands of Lieutenant Hull, who was charged to see her overhauled at the navy yard in Boston. It was a frustrat-

ing assignment, for after some months of work, orders arrived from Washington that *Constitution* was to be laid up. On 18 June 1802, *Constitution* was "put in ordinary."

Her rest was short lived. On 1 May 1803, Secretary of the Navy Robert Smith issued orders to Captain Edward Preble to proceed to Boston to "assume command of the frigate *Constitution* and have her put in a condition to sail at the shortest possible period." The new captain arrived in Boston on 19 May, and the very next day the frigate's log records:

> At 10 a.m. Commodore Preble came on board the *Constitution* and took charge as Commodore . . . Preble examined every part of the *Constitution*'s Inside & ordered a carpenter's caulking stage along side in order to examine the copper on the ship's bottom . . .

Anxious to get his frigate to sea, Preble was unsparing with his demands that the shipyard crew work longer and harder. Finally, on 14 August, *Constitution* caught a fair breeze and headed for sea.

Her destination was the Mediterranean, where the ever troublesome Barbary corsairs were once again tormenting American vessels. After a brief stop at Gibraltar, Preble set a course for the Moroccan port of Tangiers. *Constitution*'s arrival helped persuade the emperor that the United States meant to defend its trade, and on 12 October the emperor presented Preble with a personal letter to President Jefferson assuring him of Morocco's continuing friendship for the United States.

Having secured the friendship of Morocco, Preble took his frigate back to Gibraltar. A few weeks later *Constitution* left the Rock bound for Algiers to deliver the new Ameri-

can minister, Tobias Lear. After putting Lear and his entourage ashore, Preble headed once more to sea. Off Sardinia, *Constitution* was hailed by a British frigate bringing distressing news. *Philadelphia,* another American frigate, had gone aground on the Barbary coast in Tripoli harbor (now Tarabulus, on the coast of Libya), and had been captured by the Tripolitans. For *Philadelphia* to be in the hands of those pirates was intolerable. *Constitution* made for the island of Malta, where Preble might obtain the latest intelligence. At Malta Preble made the decision that since *Philadelphia* could not be retaken, she must be destroyed.

Lieutenant Stephen Decatur, captain of the American sloop of war *Enterprise,* stepped forward and offered to take the small vessel *Intrepid,* manned with a crew of volunteers, into Tripoli harbor to board and set fire to *Philadelphia.* Preble agreed, and on the evening of 16 February, *Intrepid* sailed quietly into the harbor past the sleeping Tripolitans and came alongside *Philadelphia.* Decatur and his men swarmed over the gunwales. In a few minutes of vicious hand-to-hand combat they took the frigate. Decatur's men went quickly to their sad task, and soon *Philadelphia* was a mass of flames.

Decatur's triumph convinced Preble that the time had come to "bash the Bashaw." (The "Bashaw," or pasha, was the ruler of Tripoli.) On the morning of 25 July 1804, *Constitution,* accompanied by a small squadron of other American warships, was standing off Tripoli. Five times in the next five weeks Preble assaulted the enemy. On the fourth attack, *Constitution* came within a few hundred yards of the Tripolitan fortress. She

let loose with a devastating broadside followed by another and another until, by the time she retired, her guns had poured more than three hundred shot into the fort. Inside, the Tripolitans were stunned and their guns were silent.

On his fifth and last attack, Preble brought his frigate once again to point-blank range of the enemy's guns. In a remarkable display of seamanship and gun handling, *Constitution*'s crew delivered two hundred shot in less than an hour. *Constitution*'s firepower and Preble's perseverance left the Tripolitans to ponder the wisdom of continuing their war against the United States. Early in September the "Bashaw" was dismayed to see two more American frigates heave into sight. Commodore Samuel Barron had arrived with *Constellation* and *President.* Preble welcomed Barron and, his crew weary and his frigate in need of overhaul, took *Constitution* to Malta for rest and repair.

Within a few weeks Preble was bound for home, relieved by Captain John Rodgers. *Constitution* did not go home. She was still needed.

Early in the spring the frigate was once more off Tripoli. The new captain announced her return by coming close aboard the city and firing a broadside into the town. Under Rodgers, the Americans kept the pressure on the "Bashaw," blockading the port and harassing his forces. By early June Tripoli was ready to negotiate. On 3 June 1805, representatives of the two sides met in the cabin of *Constitution.* There, on a table still visible, they signed a treaty of peace. The war with Tripoli was over.

President Jefferson was pleased with the

work his navy had accomplished. *Constitution* and her captains and crew had earned the thanks of the nation. Yet the frigate still had work to do. For several months she patrolled the Mediterranean, visiting ports to remind potential enemies of America's determination to defend her trade. Finally, on 8 August 1807, *Constitution*'s crew walked round the capstan one last time. There was joy to their effort, for as the anchor pulled free, their frigate laid a course for Boston.

Home at last, *Constitution* took up peacetime duties. In June 1810, a new captain came aboard – Isaac Hull. Although only 37 years old, Hull was a veteran officer. He had served aboard *Constitution* in action against the French during the Quasi War and had commanded *Argus* and *Enterprise* in the Mediterranean. Short and rotund (his waist measured 57 inches), Hull was an energetic and demanding captain who insisted on keeping his frigate in a high state of readiness.

Constitution was fortunate to have such an able commander at a time when the nation was once again threatened by an old enemy – Great Britain.

Relations between the United States and Great Britain had never been good. Having reluctantly granted independence, the British government followed a policy of arrogant disdain for the new republic. British forces, for example, were slow to remove themselves from American territory after the Revolution. Even after withdrawing, British officials in Canada did all they could to incite Indians to raid American frontier settlements. On the high seas the story was much the same. His majesty's navy thought nothing of interfering with American trade, even going so far as to board American ships, forcibly remove sailors, and impress them into the Royal Navy.

By the spring of 1812, resentment over British actions had reached the boiling point. On 1 June, President James Madison asked the Congress to declare war. On 18 June, the Congress of the United States declared war against Great Britain. That same day the secretary of the navy ordered *Constitution*, then at Annapolis, to sail and be prepared to "attack and capture" enemy vessels.

On 16 July *Constitution* was off the New Jersey shore, making her way northward for New York. Winds were light and Captain Hull was having difficulty holding his course. Early in the afternoon, *Constitution*'s lookout called to the deck that four sail could be seen to the north. Slowly the ships drew near. Though they were too far away to be identified, Hull suspected that they might be British. He ordered the frigate prepared for action and hoisted recognition signals. When the strangers gave no reply, Hull knew they were British. He ordered his frigate brought around and headed on a southeasterly course, away from the enemy.

The Britishers gave chase, but despite their best efforts they could not get within range of the American frigate. For three days the pursuit went on. Hull's superb seamanship and *Constitution*'s remarkable sailing qualities enabled the frigate to escape the clutches of the enemy.

A little more than one month later, *Constitution* had her second encounter with the Royal Navy. At about two in the afternoon of 19 August, *Constitution* and HMS *Guerrière*, commanded by Captain James Dacres,

sighted one another in latitude 41° 42' north and longitude 55° 48' west off the southeast shore of Nova Scotia.

Shortly after four the two frigates bore within range of one another. For nearly two hours they slugged it out. At one point in the battle a startled American seaman watched a British cannonball bounce off *Constitution*'s hull. In amazement he called out, "Huzzah, her sides are made of iron." Henceforth, this frigate would be known as "Old Ironsides."

Guerrière was no match for *Constitution*. Two hours into the battle the British frigate was a wallowing hulk. She had lost her masts and was at the mercy of the sea and wind. Dacres had no choice. *Guerrière* surrendered.

News of Hull's great victory spread through America. The people adored him and his frigate. It was with a bit of sadness, then, that shortly after he returned to Boston he asked to be given an assignment ashore. His family needed him.

Constitution's new captain, William Bainbridge, assumed command on 15 September. It took six weeks of hard labor to repair battle damage, stow provisions, and recruit men, but on 27 October, *Constitution* was once more at sea. Bainbridge set a course for the south Atlantic, and by early December *Constitution* was off Brazil.

Four days after Christmas *Constitution*'s lookouts spotted two vessels inshore, sailing in a southerly direction. One of the vessels, the larger one, apparently saw *Constitution* as well, for she changed course and made for the American; the other held her course. By 1:30 in the afternoon the stranger was close enough for Bainbridge to make an identifica-

tion. She was HMS *Java*, a frigate rated at 38 guns like her erstwhile sister *Guerrière*.

Within approximately one mile of *Java*, Bainbridge tacked, bringing *Constitution* on a parallel course with the enemy. Shortly after the two frigates were within half a mile of one another, the battle started. In the opening salvo *Constitution* took the brunt of the damage. *Java*, the faster of the pair, tried to use her speed to maneuver into a raking position; Bainbridge, however, displayed fine ship handling and managed to elude the trap. Nonetheless, *Java* did manage to deliver some savage broadsides, one of which blew away *Constitution*'s wheel. Unable to control her from the deck, Bainbridge had her steered by a jury-rigged tiller in the wardroom pantry below.

Java, too, suffered damage. On one of her attempts to rake *Constitution*, American fire carried away her jibboom. Loss of these headsails erased *Java*'s speed advantage. Her captain, Henry Lambert, fearful that *Constitution*'s heavier and more accurate fire might carry the day, decided to close and board. But as he bore down on the American, Lambert miscalculated, and the stub of his bowsprit became entangled in *Constitution*'s mizzenmast. The position was most awkward; it left *Java* exposed to *Constitution*'s main battery, but offered her no corresponding advantage.

Bainbridge took good aim, *Constitution*'s heavy guns wreaking havoc while the marines in the fighting tops sent down a hail of lead onto the Britisher's deck. In the melee, *Java* lost her foremast and main topmast. The spider's web of wreckage and debris on the deck made it even more diffi-

cult to handle the guns. *Java* was a wreck.

Bainbridge fell off to repair his own damage with the expectation of returning to force a final surrender. But aboard *Java* Captain Lambert had been wounded mortally and had been taken below. *Java*'s first lieutenant, Henry Ducie Chads, assessed the damage. Further resistance was futile; it would only mean more bloodshed. *Java* hauled down her flag.

Bainbridge surveyed the British wreck and decided she was beyond salvage. He transferred her crew and the ship's wheel to *Constitution*. The latter was a suitable replacement for the one he had lost in battle. Once more, *Constitution* came home to a hero's welcome. In less than six months she had twice bested the Royal Navy. Her fame grew.

Months at sea and the fierce encounter with *Java* had taken their toll on *Constitution*. Not until December 1813 was she fit again for sea. On the last day of that year her new captain, Charles Stewart, slipped her cable and headed south, intending to ravage the British West India trade. Stewart did well. His frigate took several merchantmen and sent many more scurrying for sanctuary in safe harbors. Not wanting to remain too long in one area lest the enemy discover him, Stewart turned north in the early spring.

On 3 April *Constitution* was off Cape Ann, headed for Boston. As she was making for the port on a southwesterly course, two large vessels sailed into view. They were the British frigates *Junon* and *Tenedos*. Hoisting every inch of canvas he could find, Stewart managed to outrun his pursuers and took refuge in Marblehead harbor. A few days later, after the British had returned to their offshore blockade, *Constitution* came around to Boston.

Stewart and his frigate spent the summer and fall trapped in their home port. The British blockaders made it too risky to try to get out. Not until 18 December was Stewart able to get *Constitution* to sea again.

Once again Stewart took his frigate south into the West Indies. He managed to take only one prize, however, and after a few weeks of cruising he decided to head into the Atlantic in hopes of finding more abundant quarry.

On 20 February 1815, at one in the afternoon, *Constitution* was sailing a southwesterly course off Madeira when a sail was sighted off the port bow. Stewart pursued, and at two a second sail came into view. The first sighting was HMS *Cyane*, a small frigate of 34 guns under the command of Captain Thomas Falcon. The second was *Levant*, a corvette of about 22 guns captained by George Douglas. Taken together, the two English ships could muster a slight edge over *Constitution* in broadside weight, but such an advantage hinged entirely on their being in complete cooperation and concert during the battle. For all practical purposes, that was an impossibility.

With a stiff breeze blowing, Stewart hoisted as much sail as possible and set out in chase. At four in the afternoon *Constitution* lost her main royal mast, causing her to take in sail and make repairs. The chase then resumed. Stewart opened fire with his bow chasers, but the range was still too extreme, and after a few ineffectual shots the guns were secured. *Levant* and *Cyane* tried to move to a windward position; failing that, they

shortened sail and went into a line formation to await *Constitution*'s arrival.

At 6:05 Stewart ranged up along the starboard side of *Cyane* and let loose with a broadside, which was ably answered by both enemies. For 15 minutes the battle raged; "then the fire of the enemy beginning to slacken and the great column of smoke clearing away we found ourselves abreast of the headmost ship, the sternmost ship luffing up for our larboard quarter." At this point Stewart was in danger of being pinned between the two. He acted quickly, pouring a broadside into the headmost ship; then, backing his sails, he moved his frigate rearward to come abreast of the sternmost ship, filling her with a broadside.

The ballet continued, with Stewart displaying extraordinary ship handling, maneuvering between the two ships while hammering them with his guns. At 6:50 *Cyane* lowered her colors, signaling surrender. Her consort lost, *Levant* headed downwind to make good her escape. By 8:00 Stewart had finished his business with *Cyane* and took up the chase. Realizing the difficulty of escape, *Levant* bravely turned to face *Constitution*. They came at each other on opposite tacks and traded broadsides. Stewart then came under her stern and raked. *Levant*'s Douglas crowded on sail and tried again to make good an escape. Her bow chasers thundering, *Constitution* took up the pursuit. The American gunners did their work skillfully and repeatedly sent well-directed shot tearing through *Levant*'s rigging. It was hopeless. At 10:00 *Levant* lowered her colors.

Stewart's victory over *Cyane* and *Levant* ranks as one of the most remarkable American naval victories ever. A fine combination of clever ship handling and expert gunnery, both the products of careful training, gave *Constitution* a well-deserved victory. There is some irony to the fact that this brilliant victory came to "Old Ironsides" after the War of 1812 was over. On Christmas eve, 1814, American and British diplomats had signed a preliminary peace in Ghent, Belgium.

Constitution's glory days were over. For nearly two decades she had fought for the infant republic. While it might be an exaggeration to say that our nation would not have survived but for *Constitution*'s victories, it is also true that the outcome of the wars with France, the Barbary States, and Great Britain might have been very different had not "Old Ironsides" been there to defend United States interests.

The American public has never forgotten *Constitution*. In 1830 a rumor spread through Boston that because of her age the Navy Department proposed to condemn the frigate. That news sparked a young Harvard student, Oliver Wendell Holmes, to write an emotional poem, "Old Ironsides."

Ay, tear her tattered ensign down!
  Long has it waved on high,
And many an eye has danced to see
  That banner in the sky;
Beneath it rung the battle shout,
  And burst the cannon's roar; –
The meteor of the ocean air
  Shall sweep the clouds no more.

Her decks once red with heroes' blood
    Where knelt the vanquished foe,
When winds were hurrying o'er the flood,
    And waves were white below,
No more shall feel the victor's tread,
    Or know the conquered knee; –
The harpies of the shore shall pluck
    The eagle of the sea!

Oh better that her shattered hulk
    Should sink beneath the wave;
Her thunders shook the mighty deep,
    And there should be her grave;
Nail to the mast her holy flag
    Set every threadbare sail,
And give her to the god of storms,
    The lightning and the gale!

Constitution was not condemned but was refitted and sent to sea. In the years to come she would see service in the Mediterranean, in the Pacific, and off the coast of Africa. During the Civil War she took up station at Newport, Rhode Island, and served as a training ship for new officers. Although the nation loved her, after the Civil War no one was sure what to do with "Old Ironsides." She went to a variety of services; finally, by 1896, the eve of her centennial, she was at the Portsmouth, New Hampshire, navy yard, where her deteriorating hull was being used as a receiving ship. Mere neglect now threatened this gallant ship more than any enemy she had ever encountered at sea.

While visiting the Portsmouth yard, John F. Fitzgerald, a Boston congressman and the grandfather of President John Fitzgerald Kennedy, saw the sad condition of the frigate. "Honey Fitz" called on his friend John D. Long, secretary of the navy, to propose a course of action. If the Congress would authorize it, would the secretary have any objection to moving *Constitution* to Boston? Secretary Long assured Fitzgerald that he had no objection. A masterful politician, Fitzgerald (later to become mayor of Boston) shepherded the legislation through Congress. In September 1897, one month before the centennial of her launching, *Constitution* was back in her old home port.

Much was still to be done, however. Years of neglect continued to take their toll. In 1925 a national campaign was undertaken to restore "Old Ironsides." Schoolchildren were encouraged to send contributions, as were other groups. Private donations combined with government appropriations were sufficient to restore the old frigate.

To celebrate her "return to service," *Constitution* was taken on a grand tour. Everywhere she went, from New York to San Francisco, people stood in line to walk her decks. She was away from Boston nearly three years, and in that time more than four and a half million people came aboard to visit. On 7 May 1934, *Constitution* came back to Boston. She has remained here ever since.

Although she was born in Boston and is berthed in Boston, USS *Constitution* is a national vessel – live oak from Georgia and South Carolina, pine from Maine, and iron from New Jersey. She deserves to be stamped "Made in America." She embodies in her timbers the skills and energy of the American men and women whose sacrifices saved the American republic. She is their monument. As she approaches her two-hundredth birthday, those who once stood on her decks might like us to think of her as a noble warrior and a gracious lady – a symbol of our nation.

William M. Fowler, Jr.

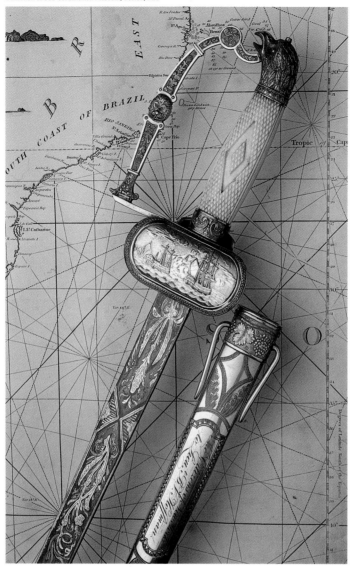

In USS Constitution Museum, one may see this historic naval officer's presentation sword and scabbard. The inscription reads as follows:

"This sword is presented by the citizens of New York to Lieut. B. V. Hoffman of the United States frigate Constitution *in testimony of his valour when assisting in the capture of the British frigate* Guerrière *on the ever memorable 18th day of August, 1812."*

Fourth Lieutenant Beekman Verplanck Hoffman served aboard *Constitution* throughout the War of 1812. He was responsible for a battery of ten 24-pounders on the after third of *Constitution*'s gun deck and participated in victories over *Guerrière, Java, Cyane,* and *Levant.* Lieutenant Hoffman was awarded three Congressional silver medals.

In the first battle between frigates in the War of 1812, *Constitution* was victorious against HMS *Guerrière*. It was during this most significant battle that a startled American gunner watched a British cannonball bounce off *Constitution*'s hull. In amazement he called out, "Huzzah, her sides are made of iron." Henceforth, this gallant frigate would be known as "Old Ironsides."

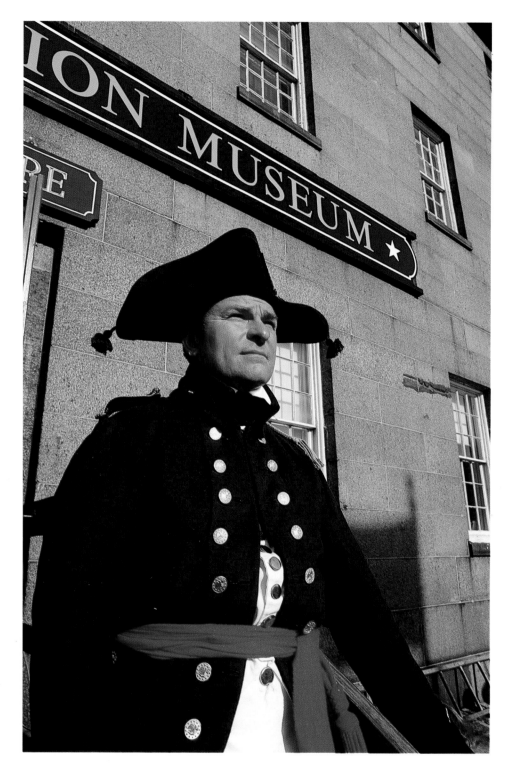
Marines were an important part of *Constitution*'s crew.

Carved and painted trail boards and a billet head decorate *Constitution*'s bow and give evidence of the craftsmanship that went into the building of this frigate.

Overleaf: *Constitution*, her decks filled with visitors, heads out into Boston Harbor for her annual turnaround cruise.

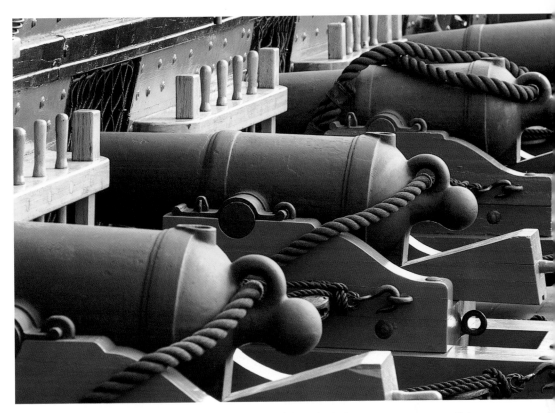

A view from aloft, looking down on *Constitution*'s spar deck. *Constitution*'s foremast rises 198 feet above her deck. Her mainmast rises 220 feet and her mizzenmast 172 feet 6 inches. She carried 42,710 square feet of sail and could reach a speed of 13 knots.

All of *Constitution*'s cannons were smooth bore and muzzle-loading. They were capable of firing a solid iron ball as well as a variety of other shot, including types intended to wound the enemy or to set fire to enemy ships and destroy their sails and rigging.

Although *Constitution* was officially described as carrying 44 guns, she often carried more than that number.

On the spar, or uppermost deck, *Constitution* carried 20 32-pound carronades. These guns weighed 2,200 pounds each and could fire a 32-pound solid shot about 400 yards. Each gun required a crew of 4 to 9 men.

One deck below, on the gun deck, the frigate mounted 32 long guns capable of firing a 24-pound shot about 1,200 yards. Each long gun weighed 5,600 pounds and required a crew of from 6 to 14 men.

In addition to the above, *Constitution* carried 2 24-pound bow chasers having an effective range of nearly 1,000 yards.

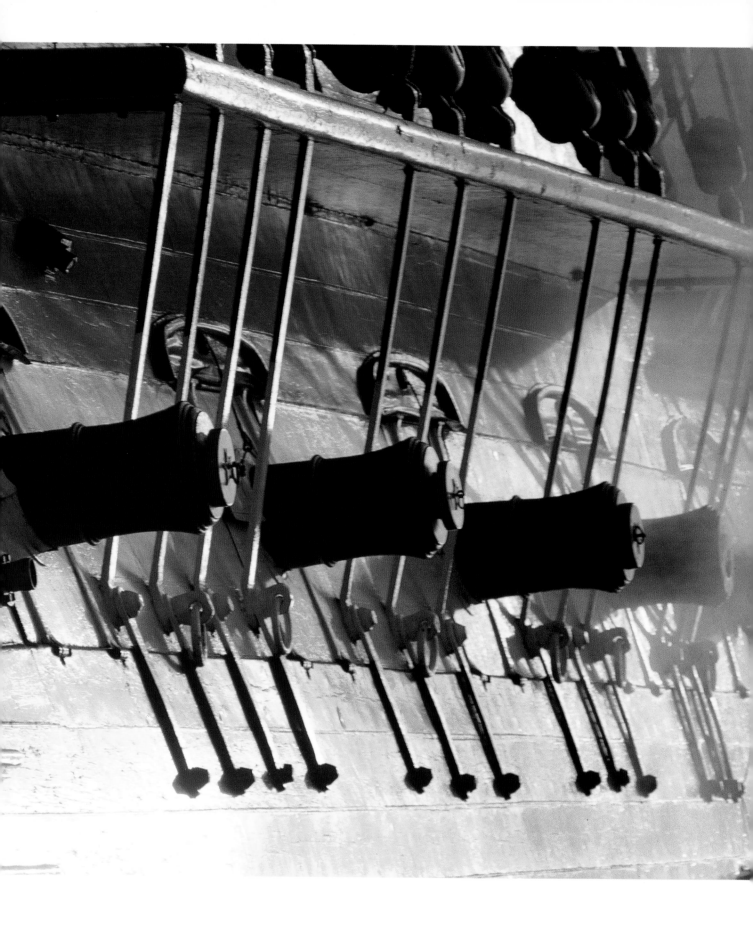

In the early morning light, *Constitution*'s 24-pounders poke through their gun ports.

English shipbuilders began the practice of carving a cat's head into the end of the stout oak beam near the bow of a ship on which the ship's heavy anchors were hoisted and secured. This process was known as "catting" the anchor and the end of the timber became known as a "cathead."

At the time *Constitution* was launched, port and starboard "catheads" were carved and gold leafed and were one of the few decorations adorning a warship of the period.

Constitution usually carried six anchors. She carried two 5,300-pound main bower anchors; a 5,400-pound sheet anchor; a 1,000-pound stream anchor; and two 400- to 700-pound kedge anchors.

Each year on the Fourth of July, *Constitution* leaves her berth at the navy yard and moves down the harbor on her annual turnaround cruise. Thousands of spectators watch from the shore as "Old Ironsides" approaches Castle Island. Abreast of the island the frigate exchanges salutes with an artillery battery, then turns around to head back to Charlestown. In 1990, in honor of the United States Coast Guard bicentennial, *Constitution* exchanged salutes with the Coast Guard barque *Eagle* and the aircraft carrier *John F. Kennedy*.

On board his ship the captain is responsible for everything. In an age when communication across oceans was measured in weeks and months, *Constitution*'s commanders had to be able to make independent decisions and carry them through with little or no advice from home. It was a solitary life.

A flintlock pistol typical of the type of side arm generally carried by officers aboard *Constitution*.

Overleaf: *Constitution* firing a morning salute.

Constitution at sunrise.

Since her commissioning nearly two centuries ago, thousands of men have served aboard *Constitution*. Her officers and enlisted men have come from all parts of America and of the world. In her fighting days she carried approximately 450 crewmen, including 55 marines and 30 boys.

Constitution is 204 feet from billet head to taffrail and 175 feet at the waterline. She has a beam of 43 feet 6 inches and displaces 2,200 tons.

Constitution remains today part of the United States Navy, and the crew aboard continue the frigate's proud traditions.

By standing on a horse block an officer was in a better position to see over the ship's bulwark.

Constitution's wheel required two to four men to control.

Marine lieutenant's stateroom.

Captain's port cabin.

"Officer country" was aft on the berthing deck. Although their staterooms were small and crowded, *Constitution*'s officers did enjoy a small degree of privacy. Enlisted men, on the other hand, who berthed forward, had virtually no privacy and were allotted only enough space to swing a hammock.

From the "fighting tops" on each mast marines could fire down on enemy decks.

A view of the spar deck, looking aft at the main hatch.

In the wardroom the ship's officers took their meals, held meetings, or simply talked together. Officer staterooms line the area.

The capstan was used to heave the anchor as well as to hoist yards and for other heavy work. After removing the ladders, the men would insert capstan bars into the square pigeonholes; then crewmen would take hold of the bars and walk around the capstan.

It was the strength of this hull that gave *Constitution* her nickname, "Old Ironsides."

Overleaf: A 24-pounder.

Constitution carried 40 to 55 marines commanded by a lieutenant or captain. The marines' mission was to help maintain order on the frigate and in battle to act as sharpshooters and boarders.

Constitution in the evening.

Fireworks over Boston Harbor illuminate "Old Ironsides."

The cooper was in charge of making and repairing all the barrels aboard ship.

A model maker at work in the USS Constitution Museum.

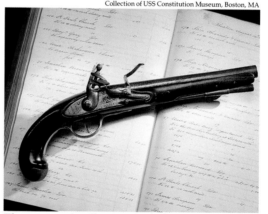

The museum's collections include weapons and manuscripts.

Only a few steps away from "Old Iron-sides" and open to the public, USS Constitution Museum houses a magnificent collection of paintings, prints, weapons, and other historic treasures relating to the history of the *Constitution*.

The captain's bottle box.

Repair and Maintenance personnel work on a new mast for *Constitution*.

USS *Constitution* Repair and Maintenance Division is housed in a building near the frigate. The task of Repair and Maintenance personnel is to keep "Old Ironsides," one of the nation's great treasures, in her historic form so that nearly one million people a year may visit and go aboard the ship.

Small craft aboard *Constitution* must also be maintained. Originally, *Constitution* carried eight small boats. She carried a 36-foot longboat, two 30-foot cutters, two 28-foot whaleboats, a 28-foot gig, a 22-foot jolly boat, and a 14-foot punt.

A Legendary Ship Continues Her Voyage…

Aside from the motion given her by the tides and the pull of a hawser, *Constitution* remained at her berth for more than a century. Although alive in the minds of her countrymen, she sat quiet and lifeless. Ships are meant to move and as this noble frigate approached her 200th birthday Americans asked "Can she still sail?"

To answer that question, technology of the twentieth century went to work on this eighteenth century machine. She was poked, prodded, and photographed. The results confirmed what those who sought to destroy her in battle had learned 200 years ago – she is well built.

To sail her though was another matter. Where are her sails? Who will man the ship? The answer to the first

question was an echo from the past. A pennies campaign was launched to buy new sails. From all over the nation people contributed. As for her crew where else to look but to our own Navy. Men and women, more accustomed to nuclear power and guided missiles, stepped forward proudly to man the yards and haul the halyards.

On the morning of July 21, 1997, "Old Ironsides", guided carefully by attending tugs, was taken into Massachusetts Bay, from a special overnight berth in Marblehead, just north of Boston. Then at the noon hour her Captain gave the order "Captain of the Deck, stand by to set sail." The towlines went slack, and for the first time in more than a century *Constitution* was sailing under her own power. "Huzzah for Old Ironsides!"

Acknowledgements

Special Thanks to:

The United States Navy

The Naval Historical Center, Washington, D.C.

Vice Admiral Joseph Metcalf III, USN (Ret), Chairman,
USS Constitution Bicentennial Planning Committee

Commander David Cashman, USN (Ret);
Lieutenant Richard Woodford, Jr., USN

Commander Christopher A. Melhuish, USN;
and the entire crew of USS Constitution

Caleb Loring, Jr.; Rear Admiral Raymond R. Couture, USNR (Ret);
Commander Leon F. Kaufman, USNR (Ret); Mrs. Robert A. Benson;
Charles F. Adams; and Dr. William M. Fowler, Jr.;
and the Trustees of the USS Constitution Museum Foundation.

Burt Logan, Director; Anne Grimes Rand, Curator;
and Christopher White, Director of Retail Operations,
USS Constitution Museum.

William Moss and the 1812 Marines

Charlie Deans and the men and women
of the Naval Historical Center Detachment, Boston

John Burchill and the staff of the
Boston National Historic Park

Llewellyn and Jay Howland for editorial
and professional guidance

Credits

Photographs Copyright © 1991 by Steve Dunwell

Copyright © 1991 by Fort Church Publishers, Inc.

Photograph page 46 Copyright © 1998
by Janet Stearns/USS Constitution Museum

All rights reserved

This book, or portions thereof, may not be reproduced
in whole or in part in any form without
the written permission of Fort Church Publishers, Inc.

Edited by James B. Patrick

Designed by Donald G. Paulhus

Published by Fort Church Publishers, Inc.,
Little Compton, Rhode Island 02837

Printed in China

Distributed by USS Constitution Museum
P.O. Box 1812
Boston, Massachusetts 02129
Tel: 617-426-1812

www.ussconstitutionmuseum.org